New Poems

D.H. Lawrence

[ZHINGOORA BOOKS]

This edition is published by
Zhingoora Books.

contact@Zhingoora.com

CONTENTS

The North Country
Bitterness of Death
Seven Seals
Reading a Letter
Twenty Years Ago
Intime
Two Wives
Heimweh
Débâcle
Narcissus
Autumn Sunshine
On That Day

APPREHENSION

AND all hours long, the town
  Roars like a beast in a cave
That is wounded there
And like to drown;
  While days rush, wave after wave
On its lair.

An invisible woe unseals
  The flood, so it passes beyond
All bounds: the great old city
Recumbent roars as it feels
  The foamy paw of the pond
Reach from immensity.

But all that it can do
  Now, as the tide rises,
Is to listen and hear the grim
Waves crash like thunder through
  The splintered streets, hear noises
Roll hollow in the interim.

COMING AWAKE

WHEN I woke, the lake-lights were quivering on the
  wall,
The sunshine swam in a shoal across and across,
And a hairy, big bee hung over the primulas
In the window, his body black fur, and the sound
  of him cross.

There was something I ought to remember: and yet I did not remember. Why should I? The run- ning lights And the airy primulas, oblivious Of the impending bee—they were fair enough sights.

FROM A COLLEGE WINDOW

THE glimmer of the limes, sun-heavy, sleeping,
  Goes trembling past me up the College wall.
Below, the lawn, in soft blue shade is keeping,
  The daisy-froth quiescent, softly in thrall.

Beyond the leaves that overhang the street,
  Along the flagged, clean pavement summer-white,
Passes the world with shadows at their feet
  Going left and right.

Remote, although I hear the beggar's cough,
  See the woman's twinkling fingers tend him a
    coin,
I sit absolved, assured I am better off
  Beyond a world I never want to join.

FLAPPER

LOVE has crept out of her sealéd heart
 As a field-bee, black and amber,
 Breaks from the winter-cell, to clamber
Up the warm grass where the sunbeams start.

Mischief has come in her dawning eyes,
 And a glint of coloured iris brings
 Such as lies along the folded wings
Of the bee before he flies.

Who, with a ruffling, careful breath,
 Has opened the wings of the wild young sprite?
 Has fluttered her spirit to stumbling flight
In her eyes, as a young bee stumbleth?

Love makes the burden of her voice.
 The hum of his heavy, staggering wings
 Sets quivering with wisdom the common
 things
That she says, and her words rejoice.

BIRDCAGE WALK

WHEN the wind blows her veil
  And uncovers her laughter
I cease, I turn pale.
When the wind blows her veil
From the woes I bewail
  Of love and hereafter:
When the wind blows her veil
I cease, I turn pale.

LETTER FROM TOWN: THE ALMOND TREE

YOU promised to send me some violets. Did you
forget?
White ones and blue ones from under the orchard
hedge?
Sweet dark purple, and white ones mixed for a
pledge
Of our early love that hardly has opened yet.

Here there's an almond tree—you have never seen
Such a one in the north—it flowers on the street,
and I stand
Every day by the fence to look up for the flowers
that expand
At rest in the blue, and wonder at what they mean.

Under the almond tree, the happy lands
Provence, Japan, and Italy repose,
And passing feet are chatter and clapping of
those
Who play around us, country girls clapping their
hands.

You, my love, the foremost, in a flowered gown,
All your unbearable tenderness, you with the
laughter
Startled upon your eyes now so wide with here-
after,
You with loose hands of abandonment hanging
down.

FLAT SUBURBS, S.W., IN THE MORNING

THE new red houses spring like plants
    In level rows
Of reddish herbage that bristles and slants
    Its square shadows.

The pink young houses show one side bright
    Flatly assuming the sun,
And one side shadow, half in sight,
    Half-hiding the pavement-run;

Where hastening creatures pass intent
    On their level way,
Threading like ants that can never relent
    And have nothing to say.

Bare stems of street-lamps stiffly stand
    At random, desolate twigs,
To testify to a blight on the land
    That has stripped their sprigs.

THIEF IN THE NIGHT

LAST night a thief came to me
  And struck at me with something dark.
I cried, but no one could hear me,
  I lay dumb and stark.

When I awoke this morning
  I could find no trace;
Perhaps 'twas a dream of warning,
  For I've lost my peace.

LETTER FROM TOWN: ON A GREY EVENING IN MARCH

THE clouds are pushing in grey reluctance slowly
northward to you,
While north of them all, at the farthest ends,
stands one bright-bosomed, aglance
With fire as it guards the wild north cloud-coasts,
red-fire seas running through
The rocks where ravens flying to windward melt
as a well-shot lance.

You should be out by the orchard, where violets
secretly darken the earth,
Or there in the woods of the twilight, with
northern wind-flowers shaken astir.
Think of me here in the library, trying and trying
a song that is worth
Tears and swords to my heart, arrows no armour
will turn or deter.

You tell me the lambs have come, they lie like
daisies white in the grass
Of the dark-green hills; new calves in shed;
peewits turn after the plough—
It is well for you. For me the navvies work in the
road where I pass
And I want to smite in anger the barren rock of
each waterless brow.

Like the sough of a wind that is caught up high in
the mesh of the budding trees,
A sudden car goes sweeping past, and I strain my
soul to hear
The voice of the furtive triumphant engine as it
rushes past like a breeze,
To hear on its mocking triumphance unwitting
the after-echo of fear.

SUBURBS ON A HAZY DAY

O STIFFLY shapen houses that change not,
  What conjuror's cloth was thrown across you,
    and raised
To show you thus transfigured, changed,
  Your stuff all gone, your menace almost rased?

Such resolute shapes, so harshly set
  In hollow blocks and cubes deformed, and heaped
In void and null profusion, how is this?
  In what strong *aqua regia* now are you steeped?

That you lose the brick-stuff out of you
  And hover like a presentment, fading faint
And vanquished, evaporate away
  To leave but only the merest possible taint!

HYDE PARK AT NIGHT, BEFORE THE WAR

Clerks.

WE have shut the doors behind us, and the velvet
flowers of night
Lean about us scattering their pollen grains of
golden light.

Now at last we lift our faces, and our faces come
aflower
To the night that takes us willing, liberates us to the
hour.

Now at last the ink and dudgeon passes from our
fervent eyes
And out of the chambered weariness wanders a
spirit abroad on its enterprise.

Not too near and not too far
Out of the stress of the crowd
Music screams as elephants scream
When they lift their trunks and scream aloud
For joy of the night when masters are
Asleep and adream.

So here I hide in the Shalimar
With a wanton princess slender and proud,
And we swoon with kisses, swoon till we seem
Two streaming peacocks gone in a cloud
Of golden dust, with star after star
On our stream.

GIPSY

I, THE man with the red scarf,
Will give thee what I have, this last week's earn-
ings.
Take them, and buy thee a silver ring
And wed me, to ease my yearnings.

For the rest, when thou art wedded
I'll wet my brow for thee
With sweat, I'll enter a house for thy sake,
Thou shalt shut doors on me.

TWO-FOLD

How gorgeous that shock of red lilies, and larkspur cleaving
All with a flash of blue!—when will she be leaving
Her room, where the night still hangs like a half-folded bat,
And passion unbearable seethes in the darkness, like must in a vat.

UNDER THE OAK

You, if you were sensible,
When I tell you the stars flash signals, each one
dreadful,
You would not turn and answer me
"The night is wonderful."

Even you, if you knew
How this darkness soaks me through and through,
and infuses
Unholy fear in my vapour, you would pause to dis-
tinguish
What hurts, from what amuses.

For I tell you
Beneath this powerful tree, my whole soul's fluid
Oozes away from me as a sacrifice steam
At the knife of a Druid.

Again I tell you, I bleed, I am bound with withies,
My life runs out.
I tell you my blood runs out on the floor of this oak,
Gout upon gout.

Above me springs the blood-born mistletoe
In the shady smoke.
But who are you, twittering to and fro
Beneath the oak?

What thing better are you, what worse?
What have you to do with the mysteries
Of this ancient place, of my ancient curse?
What place have you in my histories?

SIGH NO MORE

THE cuckoo and the coo-dove's ceaseless calling,
Calling,
Of a meaningless monotony is palling
All my morning's pleasure in the sun-fleck-scattered wood.
May-blossom and blue bird's-eye flowers falling,
Falling
In a litter through the elm-tree shade are scrawling
Messages of true-love down the dust of the high-road.
I do not like to hear the gentle grieving,
Grieving
Of the she-dove in the blossom, still believing
Love will yet again return to her and make all good.

When I know that there must ever be deceiving,
Deceiving
Of the mournful constant heart, that while she's weaving
Her woes, her lover woos and sings within another wood.

Oh, boisterous the cuckoo shouts, forestalling,
Stalling
A progress down the intricate enthralling
By-paths where the wanton-headed flowers doff their hood.

And like a laughter leads me onward, heaving,
Heaving
A sigh among the shadows, thus retrieving
A decent short regret for that which once was very good.

LOVE STORM

MANY roses in the wind
Are tapping at the window-sash.
A hawk is in the sky; his wings
Slowly begin to plash.

The roses with the west wind rapping
Are torn away, and a splash
Of red goes down the billowing air.

Still hangs the hawk, with the whole sky moving
Past him—only a wing-beat proving
The will that holds him there.

The daisies in the grass are bending,
The hawk has dropped, the wind is spending
All the roses, and unending
Rustle of leaves washes out the rending
Cry of a bird.

A red rose goes on the wind.—Ascending
The hawk his wind-swept way is wending
Easily down the sky. The daisies, sending
Strange white signals, seem intending
To show the place whence the scream was heard.

But, oh, my heart, what birds are piping!
A silver wind is hastily wiping
The face of the youngest rose.

And oh, my heart, cease apprehending!
The hawk is gone, a rose is tapping
The window-sash as the west-wind blows.

Knock, knock, 'tis no more than a red rose rapping,
And fear is a plash of wings.
What, then, if a scarlet rose goes flapping
Down the bright-grey ruin of things!

PARLIAMENT HILL IN THE EVENING

THE houses fade in a melt of mist
  Blotching the thick, soiled air
With reddish places that still resist
  The Night's slow care.

The hopeless, wintry twilight fades,
  The city corrodes out of sight
As the body corrodes when death invades
  That citadel of delight.

Now verdigris smoulderings softly spread
  Through the shroud of the town, as slow
Night-lights hither and thither shed
  Their ghastly glow.

PICCADILLY CIRCUS AT NIGHT

Street-Walkers.

WHEN into the night the yellow light is roused like
dust above the towns,
Or like a mist the moon has kissed from off a pool in
the midst of the downs,

Our faces flower for a little hour pale and uncertain
along the street,
Daisies that waken all mistaken white-spread in ex-
pectancy to meet

The luminous mist which the poor things wist was
dawn arriving across the sky,
When dawn is far behind the star the dust-lit town
has driven so high.

All the birds are folded in a silent ball of sleep,
All the flowers are faded from the asphalt isle in
the sea,
Only we hard-faced creatures go round and round,
and keep
The shores of this innermost ocean alive and
illusory.

Wanton sparrows that twittered when morning
looked in at their eyes
And the Cyprian's pavement-roses are gone, and
now it is we
Flowers of illusion who shine in our gauds, make a
Paradise
On the shores of this ceaseless ocean, gay birds of
the town-dark sea.

TARANTELLA

SAD as he sits on the white sea-stone
And the suave sea chuckles, and turns to the moon,
And the moon significant smiles at the cliffs and
  the boulders.
He sits like a shade by the flood alone
While I dance a tarantella on the rocks, and the
  croon
Of my mockery mocks at him over the waves'
  bright shoulders.

What can I do but dance alone,
Dance to the sliding sea and the moon,
For the moon on my breast and the air on my limbs
  and the foam on my feet?
For surely this earnest man has none
Of the night in his soul, and none of the tune
Of the waters within him; only the world's old
  wisdom to bleat.

I wish a wild sea-fellow would come down the
  glittering shingle,
A soulless neckar, with winking seas in his eyes
And falling waves in his arms, and the lost soul's kiss
On his lips: I long to be soulless, I tingle
To touch the sea in the last surprise
Of fiery coldness, to be gone in a lost soul's bliss.

IN CHURCH

IN the choir the boys are singing the hymn.
    The morning light on their lips
Moves in silver-moist flashes, in musical trim.

Sudden outside the high window, one crow
    Hangs in the air
And lights on a withered oak-tree's top of woe.

One bird, one blot, folded and still at the top
    Of the withered tree!—in the grail
Of crystal heaven falls one full black drop.

Like a soft full drop of darkness it seems to sway
    In the tender wine
Of our Sabbath, suffusing our sacred day.

PIANO

Softly, in the dusk, a woman is singing to me;
Taking me back down the vista of years, till I see
A child sitting under the piano, in the boom of the tingling strings
And pressing the small, poised feet of a mother who smiles as she sings.

In spite of myself, the insidious mastery of song
Betrays me back, till the heart of me weeps to belong
To the old Sunday evenings at home, with winter outside
And hymns in the cosy parlour, the tinkling piano our guide.

So now it is vain for the singer to burst into clamour
With the great black piano appassionato. The glamour
Of childish days is upon me, my manhood is cast
Down in the flood of remembrance, I weep like a child for the past.

EMBANKMENT AT NIGHT, BEFORE THE WAR

Charity.

BY the river
In the black wet night as the furtive rain slinks
down,
Dropping and starting from sleep
Alone on a seat
A woman crouches.

I must go back to her.

I want to give her
Some money. Her hand slips out of the breast of
her gown
Asleep. My fingers creep
Carefully over the sweet
Thumb-mound, into the palm's deep pouches.

So, the gift!

God, how she starts!
And looks at me, and looks in the palm of her hand!
And again at me!
I turn and run
Down the Embankment, run for my life.

But why?—why?

Because of my heart's
Beating like sobs, I come to myself, and stand
In the street spilled over splendidly
With wet, flat lights. What I've done
I know not, my soul is in strife.

The touch was on the quick. I want to forget.

PHANTASMAGORIA

RIGID sleeps the house in darkness, I alone
Like a thing unwarrantable cross the hall
And climb the stairs to find the group of doors
Standing angel-stern and tall.

I want my own room's shelter. But what is this
Throng of startled beings suddenly thrown
In confusion against my entry? Is it only the trees'
Large shadows from the outside street lamp blown?

Phantom to phantom leaning; strange women weep
Aloud, suddenly on my mind
Startling a fear unspeakable, as the shuddering wind
Breaks and sobs in the blind.

So like to women, tall strange women weeping!
Why continually do they cross the bed?
Why does my soul contract with unnatural fear?
I am listening! Is anything said?

Ever the long black figures swoop by the bed;
They seem to be beckoning, rushing away, and
 beckoning.
Whither then, whither, what is it, say
What is the reckoning.

Tall black Bacchae of midnight, why then, why
Do you rush to assail me?
Do I intrude on your rites nocturnal?
What should it avail me?

Is there some great Iacchos of these slopes
Suburban dismal?
Have I profaned some female mystery, orgies
Black and phantasmal?

NEXT MORNING

How have I wandered here to this vaulted room
In the house of life?—the floor was ruffled with gold
Last evening, and she who was softly in bloom,
Glimmered as flowers that in perfume at twilight
unfold

For the flush of the night; whereas now the gloom
Of every dirty, must-besprinkled mould,
And damp old web of misery's heirloom
Deadens this day's grey-dropping arras-fold.

And what is this that floats on the undermist
Of the mirror towards the dusty grate, as if feeling
Unsightly its way to the warmth?—this thing with
a list
To the left? this ghost like a candle swealing?

Pale-blurred, with two round black drops, as if it
missed
Itself among everything else, here hungrily stealing
Upon me!—my own reflection!—explicit gist
Of my presence there in the mirror that leans from
the ceiling!

Then will somebody square this shade with the
being I know
I was last night, when my soul rang clear as a bell
And happy as rain in summer? Why should it be
so?
What is there gone against me, why am I in hell?

PALIMPSEST OF TWILIGHT

DARKNESS comes out of the earth
  And swallows dip into the pallor of the west;
From the hay comes the clamour of children's
    mirth;
Wanes the old palimpsest.

The night-stock oozes scent,
  And a moon-blue moth goes flittering by:
All that the worldly day has meant
  Wastes like a lie.

The children have forsaken their play;
  A single star in a veil of light
Glimmers: litter of day
  Is gone from sight.

EMBANKMENT AT NIGHT, BEFORE THE WAR

Outcasts.

THE night rain, dripping unseen,
Comes endlessly kissing my face and my hands.

The river, slipping between
Lamps, is rayed with golden bands
Half way down its heaving sides;
Revealed where it hides.

Under the bridge
Great electric cars
Sing through, and each with a floor-light racing
 along at its side.
Far off, oh, midge after midge
Drifts over the gulf that bars
The night with silence, crossing the lamp-touched
 tide.

At Charing Cross, here, beneath the bridge
Sleep in a row the outcasts,
Packed in a line with their heads against the wall.
Their feet, in a broken ridge
Stretch out on the way, and a lout casts
A look as he stands on the edge of this naked stall.

Beasts that sleep will cover
Their faces in their flank; so these
Have huddled rags or limbs on the naked sleep.
Save, as the tram-cars hover
Past with the noise of a breeze
And gleam as of sunshine crossing the low black heap,

Two naked faces are seen
Bare and asleep,
Two pale clots swept and swept by the light of the
 cars.
Foam-clots showing between

The long, low tidal-heap,
The mud-weed opening two pale, shadowless stars.

Over the pallor of only two faces
Passes the gallivant beam of the trams;
Shows in only two sad places
The white bare bone of our shams.

A little, bearded man, pale, peaked in sleeping,
With a face like a chickweed flower.
And a heavy woman, sleeping still keeping
Callous and dour.

Over the pallor of only two places
Tossed on the low, black, ruffled heap
Passes the light of the tram as it races
Out of the deep.

Eloquent limbs
In disarray
Sleep-suave limbs of a youth with long, smooth
   thighs
Hutched up for warmth; the muddy rims
Of trousers fray
On the thin bare shins of a man who uneasily lies.

The balls of five red toes
As red and dirty, bare
Young birds forsaken and left in a nest of mud—
Newspaper sheets enclose
Some limbs like parcels, and tear
When the sleeper stirs or turns on the ebb of the
   flood—

One heaped mound
Of a woman's knees
As she thrusts them upward under the ruffled skirt—
And a curious dearth of sound
In the presence of these

Wastrels that sleep on the flagstones without any
hurt.

Over two shadowless, shameless faces
Stark on the heap
Travels the light as it tilts in its paces
Gone in one leap.

At the feet of the sleepers, watching,
Stand those that wait
For a place to lie down; and still as they stand,
they sleep,
Wearily catching
The flood's slow gait
Like men who are drowned, but float erect in the
deep.

Oh, the singing mansions,
Golden-lighted tall
Trams that pass, blown ruddily down the night!
The bridge on its stanchions
Stoops like a pall
To this human blight.

On the outer pavement, slowly,
Theatre people pass,
Holding aloft their umbrellas that flash and are
bright
Like flowers of infernal moly
Over nocturnal grass
Wetly bobbing and drifting away on our sight.

And still by the rotten
Row of shattered feet,
Outcasts keep guard.
Forgotten,
Forgetting, till fate shall delete
One from the ward.

The factories on the Surrey side
Are beautifully laid in black on a gold-grey sky.
The river's invisible tide
Threads and thrills like ore that is wealth to the eye.

And great gold midges
Cross the chasm
At the bridges
Above intertwined plasm.

WINTER IN THE BOULEVARD

THE frost has settled down upon the trees
And ruthlessly strangled off the fantasies
Of leaves that have gone unnoticed, swept like old
Romantic stories now no more to be told.

The trees down the boulevard stand naked in
thought,
Their abundant summery wordage silenced, caught
In the grim undertow; naked the trees confront
Implacable winter's long, cross-questioning brunt.

Has some hand balanced more leaves in the depths
of the twigs?
Some dim little efforts placed in the threads of the
birch?—
It is only the sparrows, like dead black leaves on
the sprigs,
Sitting huddled against the cerulean, one flesh with
their perch.

The clear, cold sky coldly bethinks itself.
Like vivid thought the air spins bright, and all
Trees, birds, and earth, arrested in the after-thought
Awaiting the sentence out from the welkin brought.

SCHOOL ON THE OUTSKIRTS

How different, in the middle of snows, the great
school rises red!
A red rock silent and shadowless, clung round
with clusters of shouting lads,
Some few dark-cleaving the doorway, souls that
cling as the souls of the dead
In stupor persist at the gates of life, obstinate
dark monads.

This new red rock in a waste of white rises against
the day
With shelter now, and with blandishment, since
the winds have had their way
And laid the desert horrific of silence and snow on
the world of mankind,
School now is the rock in this weary land the winter
burns and makes blind.

SICKNESS

WAVING slowly before me, pushed into the dark,
Unseen my hands explore the silence, drawing the
bark
Of my body slowly behind.

Nothing to meet my fingers but the fleece of night
Invisible blinding my face and my eyes! What if
in their flight
My hands should touch the door!

What if I suddenly stumble, and push the door
Open, and a great grey dawn swirls over my feet,
before
I can draw back!

What if unwitting I set the door of eternity wide
And am swept away in the horrible dawn, am gone
down the tide
Of eternal hereafter!

Catch my hands, my darling, between your breasts.
Take them away from their venture, before fate
wrests
The meaning out of them.

EVERLASTING FLOWERS

WHO do you think stands watching
  The snow-tops shining rosy
In heaven, now that the darkness
  Takes all but the tallest posy?

Who then sees the two-winged
  Boat down there, all alone
And asleep on the snow's last shadow,
  Like a moth on a stone?

The olive-leaves, light as gad-flies,
  Have all gone dark, gone black.
And now in the dark my soul to you
  Turns back.

To you, my little darling,
  To you, out of Italy.
For what is loveliness, my love,
  Save you have it with me!

So, there's an oxen wagon
  Comes darkly into sight:
A man with a lantern, swinging
  A little light.

What does he see, my darling
  Here by the darkened lake?
Here, in the sloping shadow
  The mountains make?

He says not a word, but passes,
  Staring at what he sees.
What ghost of us both do you think he saw
  Under the olive trees?

All the things that are lovely—
  The things you never knew—

I wanted to gather them one by one
  And bring them to you.

But never now, my darling
  Can I gather the mountain-tips
From the twilight like half-shut lilies
  To hold to your lips.

And never the two-winged vessel
  That sleeps below on the lake
Can I catch like a moth between my hands
  For you to take.

But hush, I am not regretting:
  It is far more perfect now.
I'll whisper the ghostly truth to the world
  And tell them how

I know you here in the darkness,
  How you sit in the throne of my eyes
At peace, and look out of the windows
  In glad surprise.

THE NORTH COUNTRY

IN another country, black poplars shake them-
selves over a pond,
And rooks and the rising smoke-waves scatter and
wheel from the works beyond;
The air is dark with north and with sulphur, the
grass is a darker green,
And people darkly invested with purple move
palpable through the scene.

Soundlessly down across the counties, out of the
resonant gloom
That wraps the north in stupor and purple travels
the deep, slow boom
Of the man-life north-imprisoned, shut in the hum
of the purpled steel
As it spins to sleep on its motion, drugged dense in
the sleep of the wheel.

Out of the sleep, from the gloom of motion, sound-
lessly, somnambule
Moans and booms the soul of a people imprisoned,
asleep in the rule
Of the strong machine that runs mesmeric, booming
the spell of its word
Upon them and moving them helpless, mechanic,
their will to its will deferred.

Yet all the while comes the droning inaudible, out
of the violet air,
The moaning of sleep-bound beings in travail that
toil and are will-less there
In the spell-bound north, convulsive now with a
dream near morning, strong
With violent achings heaving to burst the sleep
that is now not long.

BITTERNESS OF DEATH

I

AH, stern, cold man,
How can you lie so relentless hard
While I wash you with weeping water!
Do you set your face against the daughter
Of life? Can you never discard
Your curt pride's ban?

You masquerader!
How can you shame to act this part
Of unswerving indifference to me?
You want at last, ah me!
To break my heart
Evader!

You know your mouth
Was always sooner to soften
Even than your eyes.
Now shut it lies
Relentless, however often
I kiss it in drouth.

It has no breath
Nor any relaxing. Where,
Where are you, what have you done?
What is this mouth of stone?
How did you dare
Take cover in death!

II

Once you could see,
The white moon show like a breast revealed
By the slipping shawl of stars.
Could see the small stars tremble
As the heart beneath did wield
Systole, diastole.

All the lovely macrocosm
Was woman once to you,
Bride to your groom.
No tree in bloom
But it leaned you a new
White bosom.

And always and ever
Soft as a summering tree
Unfolds from the sky, for your good,
Unfolded womanhood;
Shedding you down as a tree
Sheds its flowers on a river.

I saw your brows
Set like rocks beside a sea of gloom,
And I shed my very soul down into your
  thought;
Like flowers I fell, to be caught
On the comforted pool, like bloom
That leaves the boughs.

III

Oh, masquerader,
With a hard face white-enamelled,
What are you now?
Do you care no longer how
My heart is trammelled,
Evader?

Is this you, after all,
Metallic, obdurate
With bowels of steel?
Did you *never* feel?—
Cold, insensate,
Mechanical!

Ah, no!—you multiform,
You that I loved, you wonderful,
You who darkened and shone,
You were many men in one;
But never this null
This never-warm!

Is this the sum of you?
Is it all nought?
Cold, metal-cold?
Are you all told
Here, iron-wrought?
Is *this* what's become of you?

SEVEN SEALS

SINCE this is the last night I keep you home,
Come, I will consecrate you for the journey.

Rather I had you would not go. Nay come,
I will not again reproach you. Lie back
And let me love you a long time ere you go.
For you are sullen-hearted still, and lack
The will to love me. But even so
I will set a seal upon you from my lip,
Will set a guard of honour at each door,
Seal up each channel out of which might slip
Your love for me.

I kiss your mouth. Ah, love,
Could I but seal its ruddy, shining spring
Of passion, parch it up, destroy, remove
Its softly-stirring crimson welling-up
Of kisses! Oh, help me, God! Here at the source
I'd lie for ever drinking and drawing in
Your fountains, as heaven drinks from out their
course
The floods.

I close your ears with kisses
And seal your nostrils; and round your neck you'll
wear—
Nay, let me work—a delicate chain of kisses.
Like beads they go around, and not one misses
To touch its fellow on either side.

And there
Full mid-between the champaign of your breast
I place a great and burning seal of love
Like a dark rose, a mystery of rest
On the slow bubbling of your rhythmic heart.

Nay, I persist, and very faith shall keep
You integral to me. Each door, each mystic port

Of egress from you I will seal and steep
In perfect chrism.
        Now it is done. The mort
Will sound in heaven before it is undone.

But let me finish what I have begun
And shirt you now invulnerable in the mail
Of iron kisses, kisses linked like steel.
Put greaves upon your thighs and knees, and frail
Webbing of steel on your feet. So you shall feel
Ensheathed invulnerable with me, with seven
Great seals upon your outgoings, and woven
Chain of my mystic will wrapped perfectly
Upon you, wrapped in indomitable me.

READING A LETTER

SHE sits on the recreation ground
 Under an oak whose yellow buds dot the pale
  blue sky.
The young grass twinkles in the wind, and the sound
 Of the wind in the knotted buds in a canopy.

So sitting under the knotted canopy
 Of the wind, she is lifted and carried away as in
  a balloon
Across the insensible void, till she stoops to see
 The sandy desert beneath her, the dreary platoon.

She knows the waste all dry beneath her, in one
  place
 Stirring with earth-coloured life, ever turning and
  stirring.
But never the motion has a human face
 Nor sound, save intermittent machinery whirring.

And so again, on the recreation ground
 She alights a stranger, wondering, unused to the
  scene;
Suffering at sight of the children playing around,
 Hurt at the chalk-coloured tulips, and the even-
  ing-green.

TWENTY YEARS AGO

ROUND the house were lilacs and strawberries
  And foal-foots spangling the paths,
And far away on the sand-hills, dewberries
  Caught dust from the sea's long swaths.

Up the wolds the woods were walking,
  And nuts fell out of their hair.
At the gate the nets hung, balking
  The star-lit rush of a hare.

In the autumn fields, the stubble
  Tinkled the music of gleaning.
At a mother's knees, the trouble
  Lost all its meaning.

Yea, what good beginnings
  To this sad end!
Have we had our innings?
  God forfend!

INTIME

RETURNING, I find her just the same,
At just the same old delicate game.

Still she says: "Nay, loose no flame
To lick me up and do me harm!
Be all yourself!—for oh, the charm
Of your heart of fire in which I look!
Oh, better there than in any book
Glow and enact the dramas and dreams
I love for ever!—there it seems
You are lovelier than life itself, till desire
Comes licking through the bars of your lips
And over my face the stray fire slips,
Leaving a burn and an ugly smart
That will have the oil of illusion. Oh, heart
Of fire and beauty, loose no more
Your reptile flames of lust; ah, store
Your passion in the basket of your soul,
Be all yourself, one bonny, burning coal
That stays with steady joy of its own fire.
But do not seek to take me by desire.
Oh, do not seek to thrust on me your fire!
For in the firing all my porcelain
Of flesh does crackle and shiver and break in pain,
My ivory and marble black with stain,
My veil of sensitive mystery rent in twain,
My altars sullied, I, bereft, remain
A priestess execrable, taken in vain—"

So the refrain
Sings itself over, and so the game
Re-starts itself wherein I am kept
Like a glowing brazier faintly blue of flame
So that the delicate love-adept
Can warm her hands and invite her soul,
Sprinkling incense and salt of words

And kisses pale, and sipping the toll
Of incense-smoke that rises like birds.

Yet I've forgotten in playing this game,
Things I have known that shall have no name;
Forgetting the place from which I came
I watch her ward away the flame,
Yet warm herself at the fire—then blame
Me that I flicker in the basket;
Me that I glow not with content
To have my substance so subtly spent;
Me that I interrupt her game.
I ought to be proud that she should ask it
Of me to be her fire-opal—.

It is well
Since I am here for so short a spell
Not to interrupt her?—Why should I
Break in by making any reply!

TWO WIVES

I

INTO the shadow-white chamber silts the white
Flux of another dawn. The wind that all night
Long has waited restless, suddenly wafts
A whirl like snow from the plum-trees and the pear,
Till petals heaped between the window-shafts
In a drift die there.

A nurse in white, at the dawning, flower-foamed pane
Draws down the blinds, whose shadows scarcely stain
The white rugs on the floor, nor the silent bed
That rides the room like a frozen berg, its crest
Finally ridged with the austere line of the dead
Stretched out at rest.

Less than a year the fourfold feet had pressed
The peaceful floor, when fell the sword on their rest.
Yet soon, too soon, she had him home again
With wounds between them, and suffering like a guest
That will not go. Now suddenly going, the pain
Leaves an empty breast.

II

A tall woman, with her long white gown aflow
As she strode her limbs amongst it, once more
She hastened towards the room. Did she know
As she listened in silence outside the silent door?
Entering, she saw him in outline, raised on a pyre
    Awaiting the fire.

Upraised on the bed, with feet erect as a bow,
Like the prow of a boat, his head laid back like the
  stern
Of a ship that stands in a shadowy sea of snow
With frozen rigging, she saw him; she drooped like
  a fern
Refolding, she slipped to the floor as a ghost-white
  peony slips
    When the thread clips.

Soft she lay as a shed flower fallen, nor heard
The ominous entry, nor saw the other love,
The dark, the grave-eyed mistress who thus dared
At such an hour to lay her claim, above
A stricken wife, so sunk in oblivion, bowed
    With misery, no more proud.

III

The stranger's hair was shorn like a lad's dark poll
And pale her ivory face: her eyes would fail
In silence when she looked: for all the whole
Darkness of failure was in them, without avail.
Dark in indomitable failure, she who had lost
        Now claimed the host,

She softly passed the sorrowful flower shed
In blonde and white on the floor, nor even turned
Her head aside, but straight towards the bed
Moved with slow feet, and her eyes' flame steadily
  burned.
She looked at him as he lay with banded cheek,
        And she started to speak

Softly: "I knew it would come to this," she said,
"I knew that some day, soon, I should find you thus.
So I did not fight you. You went your way instead
Of coming mine—and of the two of us
I died the first, I, in the after-life
        Am now your wife."

IV

"'Twas I whose fingers did draw up the young
Plant of your body: to me you looked e'er sprung
The secret of the moon within your eyes!
My mouth you met before your fine red mouth
Was set to song—and never your song denies
        My love, till you went south."

"'Twas I who placed the bloom of manhood on
Your youthful smoothness: I fleeced where fleece
  was none
Your fervent limbs with flickers and tendrils of new
Knowledge; I set your heart to its stronger beat;
I put my strength upon you, and I threw
        My life at your feet."

"But I whom the years had reared to be your bride,
Who for years was sun for your shivering, shade for
  your sweat,
Who for one strange year was as a bride to you—you
  set me aside
With all the old, sweet things of our youth;—and
  never yet
Have I ceased to grieve that I was not great enough
        To defeat your baser stuff."

V

"But you are given back again to me
Who have kept intact for you your virginity.
Who for the rest of life walk out of care,
Indifferent here of myself, since I am gone
Where you are gone, and you and I out there
        Walk now as one."

"Your widow am I, and only I. I dream
God bows his head and grants me this supreme
Pure look of your last dead face, whence now is gone
The mobility, the panther's gambolling,
And all your being is given to me, so none
        Can mock my struggling."

"And now at last I kiss your perfect face,
Perfecting now our unfinished, first embrace.
Your young hushed look that then saw God ablaze
In every bush, is given you back, and we
Are met at length to finish our rest of days
        In a unity."

HEIMWEH

FAR-OFF the lily-statues stand white-ranked in the
 garden at home.
Would God they were shattered quickly, the cattle
 would tread them out in the loam.
I wish the elder trees in flower could suddenly heave,
 and burst
The walls of the house, and nettles puff out from
 the hearth at which I was nursed.

It stands so still in the hush composed of trees and
 inviolate peace,
The home of my fathers, the place that is mine, my
 fate and my old increase.
And now that the skies are falling, the world is
 spouting in fountains of dirt,
I would give my soul for the homestead to fall with
 me, go with me, both in one hurt.

DEBACLE

THE trees in trouble because of autumn,
  And scarlet berries falling from the bush,
And all the myriad houseless seeds
  Loosing hold in the wind's insistent push

Moan softly with autumnal parturition,
  Poor, obscure fruits extruded out of light
Into the world of shadow, carried down
  Between the bitter knees of the after-night.

Bushed in an uncouth ardour, coiled at core
  With a knot of life that only bliss can unravel,
Fall all the fruits most bitterly into earth
  Bitterly into corrosion bitterly travel.

What is it internecine that is locked,
  By very fierceness into a quiescence
Within the rage? We shall not know till it burst
  Out of corrosion into new florescence.

Nay, but how tortured is the frightful seed
  The spark intense within it, all without
Mordant corrosion gnashing and champing hard
  For ruin on the naked small redoubt.

Bitter, to fold the issue, and make no sally;
  To have the mystery, but not go forth;
To bear, but retaliate nothing, given to save
  The spark in storms of corrosion, as seeds from
    the north.

The sharper, more horrid the pressure, the harder
    the heart
  That saves the blue grain of eternal fire
Within its quick, committed to hold and wait
  And suffer unheeding, only forbidden to expire.

NARCISSUS

WHERE the minnows trace
A glinting web quick hid in the gloom of the brook,
When I think of the place
And remember the small lad lying intent to look
Through the shadowy face
At the little fish thread-threading the watery nook—

It seems to me
The woman you are should be nixie, there is a pool
Where we ought to be.
You undine-clear and pearly, soullessly cool
And waterly
The pool for my limbs to fathom, my soul's last
school.

Narcissus
Ventured so long ago in the deeps of reflection.
Illyssus
Broke the bounds and beyond!—Dim recollection
Of fishes
Soundlessly moving in heaven's other direction!

Be
Undine towards the waters, moving back;
For me
A pool! Put off the soul you've got, oh lack
Your human self immortal; take the watery track.

AUTUMN SUNSHINE

THE sun sets out the autumn crocuses
  And fills them up a pouring measure
  Of death-producing wine, till treasure
Runs waste down their chalices.

All, all Persephone's pale cups of mould
  Are on the board, are over-filled;
  The portion to the gods is spilled;
Now, mortals all, take hold!

The time is now, the wine-cup full and full
  Of lambent heaven, a pledging-cup;
  Let now all mortal men take up
The drink, and a long, strong pull.

Out of the hell-queen's cup, the heaven's pale wine—
  Drink then, invisible heroes, drink.
  Lips to the vessels, never shrink,
Throats to the heavens incline.

And take within the wine the god's great oath
  By heaven and earth and hellish stream
  To break this sick and nauseous dream
We writhe and lust in, both.

Swear, in the pale wine poured from the cups of the
    queen
  Of hell, to wake and be free
  From this nightmare we writhe in,
Break out of this foul has-been.

ON THAT DAY

ON that day
I shall put roses on roses, and cover your grave
With multitude of white roses: and since you were
brave
One bright red ray.

So people, passing under
The ash-trees of the valley-road, will raise
Their eyes and look at the grave on the hill, in
wonder,
Wondering mount, and put the flowers asunder

To see whose praise
Is blazoned here so white and so bloodily red.
Then they will say: "'Tis long since she is dead,
Who has remembered her after many days?"

And standing there
They will consider how you went your ways
Unnoticed among them, a still queen lost in the
maze
Of this earthly affair.

A queen, they'll say,
Has slept unnoticed on a forgotten hill.
Sleeps on unknown, unnoticed there, until
Dawns my insurgent day.

The End

CPSIA information can be obtained at www.ICGtesting.com
Printed in the USA
LVOW05s1751140414

381651LV00030B/1018/P

9 781479 198184